Gay Husbands Say the Darndest Things

BY

Bonnie Kaye, M.Ed.

CCB Publishing
British Columbia, Canada

Gay Husbands Say the Darndest Things

Copyright © 2013 by Bonnie Kaye, M.Ed.
ISBN-13: 978-1-77143-093-7
First Edition

Library and Archives Canada Cataloguing in Publication
Kaye, Bonnie, 1951-, author
Gay husbands say the darndest things / by Bonnie Kaye. -- First edition.
Issued in print and electronic formats.
ISBN 978-1-77143-093-7 (pbk.).--ISBN 978-1-77143-094-4 (pdf)
Additional cataloguing data available from Library and Archives Canada

Cover artwork by Andrea Brower: apbpersonal@gmail.com

Publisher: CCB Publishing
               British Columbia, Canada
               www.ccbpublishing.com

DEDICATION

To the women who have listened
to these "DARNDEST" things for years

To the wonderful members of my Straight Wives Club
who contributed the materials in the book
to help guide other women into the light

And to the many women who will find the strength
in the future to realize that you can take back your life

Contents

Introduction

In this country, there are over 4 million women who are or were married to gay men. Throughout the world, there are millions of more women in this situation especially in countries and cultures where homosexuality is discriminated against to the point of death. Even though the numbers are certainly high, each woman who travels this path feels extremely isolated as if she is the only one in this situation.

Why is this so isolating? Namely because no woman is celebrating the fact that the man she married for the rest of her life is out there pursuing other men. This is not a proud event where you send out announcements. It is one that is clothed in secrecy for fear of shame, blame, and accusations of stupidity. The stigma of "gay" may be changing in the world today, but the stigma of "straight wife" is way behind in acceptance and is not catching up at all.

When women come to me and tell me that they feel "stupid" for not knowing that the man they married is gay, I am the first to tell them that it is not a matter of "stupid." It's a matter of "uneducated." We grew up in a society that taught us that "gay" means "same." It is defined in the dictionary as such. I remember learning as a teenager about "homosexuals" and how the male ones were attracted to men while the women only wanted other women to be with.

I grew up in the 1960's. In 1968 when I was in my late teens, I moved to California where I had the opportunity to meet numerous gay men who were out (for the most part) and content living a gay life. At the age of 18, I remember developing a giant crush on one, Glen, age 23. He was adorable, personable, and very flamboyant. He had a younger boyfriend, Larry, who was 19, and an older sugar daddy, Roger, who was 45. This was a world totally foreign to me.

When I met Glen, he was the first openly gay man I had ever encountered. I asked myself why would he want to be gay? He probably didn't have a mother who loved him enough, so this is his way of rebelling. Boy, was I stupid. I believed if Glen had a woman to love him, those thoughts for men would go away. I pursued him in hopes of "fixing" him.

Ironically, he really liked me as a close friend. We actually had unsuccessful sexual encounters on three different occasions. Look, it was the 1960's in California where sex was defined the generation. We became such good friends that Glen even asked me to go with him to Mexico to get married. We both considered it for about three hours, but then we decided not to do it, saving ourselves from getting a divorce. We both knew whatever wonderful feelings we had for each other as friends would quickly dissolve if we tried to play "house" together. It was a momentary fantasy. He wanted to have the straight dream of a wife and children for a short moment, and I wanted to get married and have someone to love for a lifetime.

I learned from that experience that a gay man and a straight woman could never be happily married. The difference was that *I knew he was a gay man* because he was *openly gay*. There was no hiding; he proudly walked down the street arm in arm with his boyfriend Larry. In 1968 in Southern California, this was not such a unique sight. Even though his "sugar daddy" Roger was

2

parading in the suit of a respectable "straight" bachelor accountant, when he was with Glen, it just seemed natural. I didn't have a hard time conceiving Roger was gay although he didn't have the stereotypical effeminate behaviors that Glen and Larry had. At least Roger never married.

It was quite different when I met my gay husband eight years later. There was nothing apparently gay about him; in fact, he was quite the opposite. He was a man of strength. He taught kung-fu, a very dangerous martial art. He had many women surrounding him vying for his attention. We had sex early in the relationship. He wasn't the best in bed, but I certainly had worse than him in the past. He claimed that he had numerous sexual experiences, and there was no reason for me to even slightly suspect that they were gay sexual experiences at that point. But even if I had found out that my ex-husband had "gay sex" in the past, I still would have married him. Why? Because back in the 1970's, we were still in the midst of a "sexual revolution" where many people tried everything. I would have thought that he tried it--and didn't like it--so he's straight.

Does that sound ridiculous? Well, it's not. I went with a man prior to my gay husband where that was the case. Rick was a former high school sweetheart with whom I had an on-again, off-again relationship with over a span of eight years. In between, I married for the first time and lost touch. After the first marriage failed at the age of 25, I got in touch with him. By this time he was a doctor living in Massachusetts, and I was living in New York City. We decided to meet again and catch up on the past five years since our last time together.

During that evening, Rick told me about two relationships he had with men after college, followed by two relationships he had with women. He knew that he wasn't gay at that point, and his sexuality was heterosexual. Yep--the "I tried it and didn't like it" theory that rang through my head. We rekindled our relationship which went on for nearly seven months.

Once again, as in the past, something was off. We had sex, but it always felt "empty" as if something was missing. He was there with me physically, but not really there mentally. The fact that he wanted to have sex with me meant to me that he was straight. I broke up the relationship at that point because he wanted more than I could give in terms of commitment, but I kept in touch with him by phone for a number of years. One day when I called his house and a man answered, my gut instinct told me he was now gay.

Of course that "gut instinct" came after the end of my own marriage to a gay man and running a support group for a few years that opened my eyes to these realities. When I asked Rick if he was gay, he told me, "Yes." When I asked if that was his partner who answered the phone, he said yes again.

I then questioned myself how I had no clue that I was in two major relationships with gay men. I learned over time that there was no way I could tell that these men were gay because they were trying so hard every day to "act straight." They were determined not to be part of a world that was being called deviant and perverted. They wanted what all of us want—love, respect, and acceptance. They believed that marriage would provide all of these--and it did. What it couldn't provide was happiness. Why? Because they are gay.

I tell our women that when gay men marry you, in almost all cases they do love you. But they love you to the **BEST OF THEIR ABILITIES TO LOVE AS GAY MEN**. And yes, there is a major difference between gay love and straight love from a man. Ask any woman who has been with both and she will tell you that. Gay men are "visitors" in a marriage rather than "participants." They do what they have to do in order to get by and not raise the red flags and wave them in your face--but trust me, it is an act. It all comes down to how long the show can go on before they get tired of playing the role.

Gay men who marry can have sex with their wives--at least at first. They will do it because it's expected in the beginning of the marriage, but in most cases, it won't be long until those feelings (a) diminish, and (b) then become a chore, and (c) finally become impossible and (d) even repulsive. Rather than tell their wives the truth, they will disguise it in a number of ways ranging from headaches, backaches, toothaches, stress from work, stress from the kids, stress from financial matters, and stress from living in a world that is always creating hardships for them--namely you!

In reality, it is the stress of being a gay man stuck in a straight marriage and trying to get his penis "pumped up" when he needs to make it work for a woman. These men can blame their broken penises on Low T, Erectile Dysfunction, depression, stress, sickness, and medication. If that were true, why are they foaming over gay porno on the computer, masturbating, and buying little blue pills that they aren't using with you? What about the packs of condoms that mysteriously disappear while you are NOT having sex with them?

After working with over 90,000 women over the past 30 years, the number one issue that the majority of our women wrestle with is the lack of evidence or proof that their husbands are gay. My advice of "Trust your instincts" doesn't appeal to many of them who are raising families and who took vows to stick in there through better or worse till death do they part.

5

In my research through the years, I have learned that nearly 60% of gay men in marriages to women will NEVER tell them the truth for a variety of reasons which include:

1. Their fear of their homosexuality being discovered by their family members

2. Their fear of repercussions from their wife and children

3. Their belief that they can never fit into the gay community because they don't fit the "gay image"

4. Their refusal to believe that they are gay because they don't want to be gay.

Now that last one may seem ridiculous to you, but trust me, this is a major factor with many of our gay husbands. These men honestly believe they are *not* gay. They do not equate having sex with men as "gay." They don't want to risk what they have as far as security of a family over sex with a man. Besides, if they were gay, why do they love their wives and children? Gay men don't have attractions to women--only to men. And since he is married to you, that proves he is attracted to women--even if he doesn't want to be intimate with you. I do get kind of lost at this point, but these husbands keep believing that line!

I am no longer calling this **"Denial."** I am calling this **"Justification**." Justification is when you know you're doing the gay thing but prefer to call it something different like, "experimentation," "straight with issues," or the newest term "heteroflexible."

Guess what? Straight Guys are not doing these things. I tell our women to wake up and learn to trust their instincts. If your husband can't accept he is gay, then you accept it. If he wants to live in denial, then let him. You don't have to sail down that river with him. Let him yell, deny, blame you, justify, disguise, and lie--it changes nothing. He is gay, and the sooner YOU accept that, the sooner you can move on with your life.

My goal in putting this book together was simple. I wanted other women who were once in your shoes of not knowing the truth to give you a list of red flags of things their gay husbands said to throw them off track. I remember when I was married to my gay husband how dehumanized I felt. His frustration of living in a straight marriage rapidly tore away at my self-esteem as a woman. Even though on an intellectual level I knew the problems weren't what he accused me of, emotionally I was torn up inside believing there was something wrong with me. After all, if my husband was so "unhappy" and feeling "trapped," I obviously was doing something wrong.

I spent a lot of time trying to "improving" myself so I could make him love me the way I needed to be loved. Nothing worked. There was always something I was doing wrong. And if I wasn't doing something wrong when he felt frustrated, he would drag up things that happened before to make me feel worse. I felt like those gerbils running around the wheel and going nowhere but on an exhausting journey.

The problem for the majority of women who are stuck is you are waiting for a confession that is NEVER coming. You try every approach to get your husbands to admit the truth--but they don't. I used to think they just lied about this to protect themselves. I have come to realize that in many cases they lie about it to you

because they are lying to themselves. They can't accept they are gay. They will justify their sexual behaviors in every way except gay. Some of them are scared--others are just cowards.

My hope is that women who are doubting their husbands' homosexuality because of the chronic denials will now realize after reading the comments made to other straight wives what the truth is. It is almost as if there is a "Gay Husbands' School of Lies." For sure, there is a network on line because a number of us have found various Internet sites that do this. I also hope this saves you years of self-doubt and self-blame for something that you have no control over. As I tell our women, "You didn't create it--you can't change it. You can only learn to accept it and move on and save yourself."

Several years ago, in September 2011, I wrote this article for my monthly newsletter "Bonnie Kaye's Straight Talk." I would like to share it with you in the spirit it was written in:

GAY HUSBANDS SAY THE DARNDEST THINGS!

In the thousands of letters for help or support I receive each year, at least half of them are from women who HAVE NO PROOF. They have a gut feeling, but they don't trust it. That's because their sense of reality has been "slip slidin' away" from the chaos and confusion their husbands have been putting them through. Most of these guys are one step ahead of you, and even when you catch up or get one step in front of them, they find a way to trip you up so you slide back again. It's not easy always having to be one step ahead of someone who is trying to "gaylight" you.

Sometimes a woman does get a partial admission such as, "I am just looking at pictures—I would never act on it," or "I'm just comparing myself to other men to see how I 'stack up'." Even though there is *half a sigh* of relief when you hear these ridiculous explanations--which I guess is better than *none*--you still feel out of sorts. Once the doubt is there, you can only stay in "ostrich mode" for so long. You can keep your head buried, but sooner or later when the next picture of pornography pops up on the computer, you have a harder time burying your head in the sand deeper than it already is.

For those of you who just can't seem to get the proof you need that your husband is gay, I decided to request information from my online support group members asking them to share with us the excuses their husbands would give them for not making love to them in a meaningful way on a regular basis. I thought maybe if you could connect with some of these reasons, you would have that long awaited "ah hah" moment to put you on the right track.

So, with a slight drum roll, here are some of the top 50 excuses our women sent me:

1. I turn him off because I ask for it. By the way, I only ask maybe once a month.

2. All you think about is sex.

3. He says it's not a perfect world, and I can't have everything.

4. He hates the smell of a woman.

5. He took medication so he can't have sex with me.

6. He was busy and he wasn't having sex with me.

7. He is too tired.

8. I asked him if he wanted oral sex, but he said he wasn't in the mood.

9. I came home from work early to surprise him thinking we might have sex, but he said, "Don't ever come home without calling first ever again!"

10. He told me I was a nymphomaniac.

11. When I kissed his neck and his said ear, he said, "Stop, that makes me sick, I don't like that!

12. He told me if I would stick around, I might get it.

13. Said he just took a shower ...he can't have sex now.

14. His back hurts.

15. He's too busy.

16. He doesn't like sex at night.

17. I'm too mean.

18. I'm too fat.

19. He's too tired.

20. I'm too pushy.

21. "If you would clean up the house, I would"

22. "You know watching you cook and clean turns me on."

23. You're too big.

24. You want it too much.

25. He compared my body to other women and told me what he liked about them better...if you had bigger nipples, etc.

26. You look too much like a Rick James.

27. "It" is too worn out...you use that vibrator too much.

28. You wait until it's too late.

29. It's too early.

30. "It's broke" was his favorite line.

31. When I would ask for a hug he's say "nah, I don't feel like it right now."

32. Give me time, and it will come back to me. Those were two lines I heard forever.

33. "We are not sexual creatures": His favorite mantra for the last years of our marriage.

34. "I have a urinary infection": Used this excuse the last years of our marriage.

35. "Too tired, got to get up early and go to work. I have a real job:" He said this one a lot, especially during the last years of the marriage.

36. "I no longer find you attractive," said 6 weeks after our second and last child was born (1996). I begged him to make love to me. He stated, "No. I no longer find you attractive." I swore I would never beg for sex again. After our son was born, we had sex once every 3 years.

37. "You stink." Said this the night our son was conceived. I was starting foreplay. He stopped me and said, "You stink" and then turned his back to me. I quietly cried myself to sleep. I was suddenly awakened when he forcefully whipped my body around so I was on my back. He forced himself in me. It lasted less than a minute. All our sexual encounters lasted about a minute or two and they all ended with him turning his back to me.

He never brought me to an orgasm. He never cuddled or held me as we slept.

38. "Our daughter will hear us and I don't want to wake her." He said this a few times early in the marriage.

39. "I'm sea sick." Our Honeymoon. He did not make love to me until the end of our honeymoon.

40. "Going down to the bar to hang out with the guys. Be right back." He said this on our wedding night. I was shocked that he would leave his bride and cried myself to sleep. He did not come right back, and I did not go looking for him. His stall tactic worked. We did not make love on our wedding night.

41. Having sex with you is "boring." You don't do anything exciting.

42. All people slow down with sex after they are married for a while.

43. You don't have enough experience in bed to satisfy me.

44. You have terrible breath, so I can't stand to kiss you.

45. You are too flat-chested.

46. You need to have a breast reduction.

47. Your body is sagging.

48. You aren't willing to use toys with me.

49. You don't have a good sexual technique and you can't learn that.

50. You don't know how to please a man.

And now, the comprehensive compilation of excuses from some of the women in our network! If you check off the ones you hear in your marriage, and look at them all at the end of the book, no doubt, you'll see your life. Do you know how I know that? Women with straight husbands would never think to buy this book!

Gay Husbands Say the Darndest Things

The following pages are written

by the women in the

Straight Wives Club

Gay Husbands Say the Darndest Things

From Beth

From him:

- ✓ "I am the victim here."
- ✓ "If we divorce, I will lose your health insurance."
- ✓ "I am taking Cialas so we can have better sex."
- ✓ "I have to work late."
- ✓ "I have to go out of town for work."
- ✓ I said, "Why don't you come to bed with me?" His reply: "Because I have work I need to get done."
- ✓ Comment I read from an email from one of his partners: "We need to make sure we have sex with our wives tonight, so they don't suspect anything."

From Kelly

✓ He said his fantasy life was "natural, healthy and normal and you can accept it or we're done." (meaning the marriage was over). This was before I filed for divorce and he found God.

✓ He spent hours digging up research online trying to convince me that many or most men fantasize about sex with men. I told him I wasn't impressed with his radical, secular sources.

✓ He told me my not wanting to stay married to him because of his bisexuality was "no different than discrimination against Blacks in the 50's," thereby essentially calling me a bigot. Nice.

✓ He also equated my discovery of his sexuality to other life events that spouses are supposed to love each other through. I am at high risk for breast cancer due to family history. He said he would not walk away from me if I develop breast cancer, so I should not leave him because I discovered he is ...."bisexual." Really? I thought about asking him if he thought his sexuality was an illness, but I restrained myself. Now I kind of wish I hadn't!

✓ After I filed for divorce, he suddenly found God. This from the man who earlier in the marriage tried to talk me out of my practice of going to church every Sunday. He said God wanted us to be married. He said God has a plan for us. He made me listen to an online sermon from his childhood pastor talking about how God's plans for us are bigger than our plans for ourselves and basically how we need to shelve our plans for ourselves so we can be open to God's plans for us. So he was using this sermon and his pastor to try to coerce me to stay in the marriage. He said God works miracles. I think he was insinuating that God would cure him of his homosexuality. I think he is currently trying to pray it away. I told him to leave God out of it because he would not like what God had to say on the matter.

✓ He told me "If you have to put a label on me, I would say I'm bisexual." Later he retracted that. He said he couldn't even remember what he told me in that initial conversation. Later, he told me "I'm not *that* gay." And, of course, "I'm not gay."

✓ He told me he fantasized about men giving him oral sex but he never fantasized about having sex with men. Huh? Duh, even teenagers these days know oral sex is sex! Oh, this was many months before I found all the downloaded gay porn which included photos of anal sex. So that was a bald faced lie as well. You view and download photos of men engaged in anal sex but you don't fantasize about having sex with men? Really?

✓ I took an old computer in to the shop to have it mined for what was on it. I found 5 1/2 years of downloaded gay porn. Not a woman to be seen anywhere. The downloads included 128 photos which took place on 28 different occasions from 1997-2003, the period that he used this particular computer. I had our second child in 1997 and our third in 2000. While I was pregnant, enduring pre-term labor with contractions every 7-8 minutes for months on end, nursing newborns, experiencing sleep deprivation, he was downloading gay porn, fantasizing about sex with men and pleasuring himself.

✓ The juxtaposition of the reality of our two lives sickens me. I was 100% committed to our life, our family and he was completely self-absorbed. I have thought of putting together a slide show, (would love to be able to use it in court), showing pictures of me pregnant, holding my babies, interspersed with photos of the gay porn he was viewing at the time. I think that would paint a vivid picture of the reality of what went on here. I found more searches in 2010 and 2011, so the picture of what he was up to on a regular basis throughout our marriage becomes quite clear.

✓ He did tell me he has sexual thoughts throughout the day every day and some of them include men. He said he cannot control these thoughts.

✓ He told me he wished I was more adventurous in bed. Again, insinuating that his ventures to the dark side were related to my lack of sexual adventure. I didn't fall for that one.

✓ He talked about his gay porn habit and fantasy life as being related to the timing of the birth of our 4th child, like somehow I was so involved with her I didn't pay him enough attention, so he sought what he needed in his fantasy life. He even cried when telling me this one. Again, incredible spinning because she was born in 2006 and I have evidence dating back to 1997, plus his admission that he has "always been this way" meaning sexually attracted to men and he knew it before we married in 1992.

✓ I think about the pain of my betrayal and I still don't have any evidence that he ever chatted with anyone or hooked up with a man ever. He might have. He might not have. I may never know.

✓ The betrayal is still so stunningly painful. I do believe it would be worse if I knew more but on some levels, it is hard to imagine it would/could be much worse. I know if he did not "act out", then I am fortunate compared to what many straight wives have had to endure, but this is enough for me. It is still such a crazy betrayal of our marriage and our family and my fidelity.

From Suz

I remember him saying all the time:

- ✓ "It's not cheating if it's with the same sex."
- ✓ "It's not cheating if I tell you about it."
- ✓ "Why don't you find a woman you can date - that would be okay and we would still be monogamous." Remember it's not cheating if your with the same sex.
- ✓ I would always joke with my friends (laughter sometimes helped) I thought he asked me to love him till he was old and gray not old and gay!

From Rosemary

Now I remember my husband's words ringing in my ears:

✓ **"I'm not gay. Just.....PASSIVE"**! And he was. Both.

From Beth

- ✓ It was hard to accept that your husband of 34 years (Okay - I will say 22 years - since that is when I first suspected that he was gay), cares more about his penis than his wife.

- ✓ I have accepted it - and I am doing what I need to do - seeing a therapist, reading your newsletters, obtaining a divorce.

- ✓ My gay husband denies that he is gay. I knew that he was both placing ads and cruising Craigslist to find men. When I confronted him about it - he said "Craigslist doesn't work. I place ads out there and hardly anyone responds, and I answer a lot of ads and they hardly ever get back to me. So you can't accuse me of arranging hookups using Craigslist."

- ✓ It took me years to finally admit to myself that he wasn't going to change, that he doesn't want to change, and his penis is so much more important to him than his wife or his two adult children. I am finally in the process of obtaining a divorce.

From Jen

✓ "It didn't mean anything - it was just oral."

✓ "It's a refurbished computer, those 'male escort' searches were probably done by the person who owned the computer before me."

✓ "I'm under a lot of stress. Going to the bathhouse was a way to relieve stress. It's just a stress reliever, I'm not gay."

✓ "I'm not gay, I went to male bathhouses because female bathhouses don't exist. If I could have gone to a bathhouse filled with women, I would have much preferred that."

Kind of funny to think about that now - did he actually think a female bathhouse would have made me feel any better?.......rhetorical question obviously!

From Amy

- ✓ I love you, but I don't know how I love you.
- ✓ I don't want a divorce. We can stay married and just start new chapters in our lives.
- ✓ I am not gay. You are crazy and delusional again.
- ✓ I think I am dying. You cannot leave me.
- ✓ If you leave me, I will make sure no one ever loves you again.
- ✓ We would still be together if it wasn't for you.
- ✓ If you leave, I will make your children hate you someday.
- ✓ My friend is not gay. Now you have emasculated me.
- ✓ You distorted the children's perceptions of me; I am not gay.
- ✓ I am not gay. You are a lesbian. (LOL) I know you had an affair with one of your girlfriends.
- ✓ From the husband's family: This all happened because you are a slut.
- ✓ I am the good one. My family is bad. I am the black sheep of the family.
- ✓ Please just let me go on this vacation with a man quietly. I promise I will come back a better husband.
- ✓ You don't defend me anymore.
- ✓ People say I am gay because they are jealous of me and envious. They see we have a good marriage and want to destroy it.
- ✓ I was not caught naked with that man. I was wearing a three piece suit. (LOL)

- ✓ We are just friends. Please be friends with his wife. They have a marriage just like ours. (Sure they did!!)
- ✓ You are controlling and jealous.
- ✓ I am not that debonair man you speak of. What do I have--the doppelganger affect?
- ✓ I am going on the Amazing Race with a friend for 45 days. But he is just a "friend."
- ✓ While dressed in women's clothing for Halloween, he stated, "I really thought I would be more beautiful."
- ✓ Do these pants make my waste look big? (While weighing about 150 after 70 pounds of weight loss.)
- ✓ If you join the gym, I will quit. But in the meantime, he called me fat and out of shape.
- ✓ You have to trust me.
- ✓ You are disloyal.
- ✓ You signed a contractual agreement to be loyal to me for the rest of your life.
- ✓ The computer has a virus. It wasn't me. My friend was looking up perverted porn. (That's how all the computers got penises on them.)
- ✓ You have given me all of my moral values and if it were for you I wouldn't have any.
- ✓ I'm a Republican. (While having affairs with men and Democratic Party members and donating to them in all ways including financial.)
- ✓ You can never divorce me.
- ✓ I don't know where my wedding ring went. I told you I lost it months ago in the sink at a football game.
- ✓ I don't know where your engagement ring went but it will never be found.

✓ No one will ever love you.

✓ My cell phone stopped working and wouldn't hold a charge.

✓ I slept at the office last night again.

✓ These are not my friends, they are all your friends. (Distancing from friends.)

✓ To Police: She is playing games again. (All the while he refuses to return our son to me during Court ordered parenting time.)

✓ I have a spending problem because you made me unhappy. (LOL)

✓ You are not allowed to go food shopping because you are too cheap.

✓ I was too drunk and had to pull to the side of the road overnight. Don't you want your husband to be safe!!!

✓ You hindered me from my religion and from being a good Catholic.

✓ If you are a good mother, you will stay.

✓ Give me three more months and I will figure it all out. (Heard this 100s of times)

✓ I've got it all under control!!!!

✓ I forgot I was watching the baby. I went to the golf course.

✓ He likes Michael Jackson just like me.

From Gill

Things my husband has said.

- ✓ It was just once to try it and see if I liked it. I don't think it is for me and won't happen again. (2003) Then in 2007 through to 20012, "I have had several. I am not sure I did enough to know. I only received--I have not given."
- ✓ He made three visits to a sauna and claims only touching was involved.
- ✓ "I am not gay--I just want anal activity."
- ✓ He has used toys on himself since late teens. He says he only fantasies about women so cannot be gay.

From Danel

- ✓ "I'm not going to live with a guy," like pass the popcorn and where's the remote?

From Colleen

✓ While intoxicated, my husband was sleep talking. He kept saying, "Put your balls in my mouth." The next morning I asked him what he was dreaming about .... He looked me dead in the eye and said, "Only you, only you!" I never told him what he said.

From Laura

- ✓ "I did it to make sure I wasn't gay, and I'll never do it again."
- ✓ "This is between us only, and you must not tell anyone."
- ✓ "I am not a gay man!!!"
- ✓ "I did it because I have a 'Comparison Issue.'"
- ✓ "I keep that photo from the Men's Fitness magazine in my bathroom drawer because it motivates me to lose weight."
- ✓ "I'm going to the gym to work out."
- ✓ "I need the lights off because I'm afraid someone might see in." (Even though the curtains are closed).
- ✓ "I don't want you touching me because I can't fall asleep."
- ✓ "You'll never make it being alone."
- ✓ The Mother-In-Law from hell saying to me, "You need to take some responsibility for all this."
- ✓ The Father-In-Law from hell saying to me, "I guess we never really knew you, and this is your fault."

From Annette

- ✓ When marriage counseling with our minister, he gave his reason for counseling and (supposed) self - examination, "I don't want to have another ex-wife."
- ✓ When I caught him in a lie, he shouted, "Yeah, I lied. What are you going to do about it?"
- ✓ When I attempted to hold him accountable for a promise he'd made, he said matter of fact, "I lied."
- ✓ He said, more or less out of the blue, "I don't think I ever bonded with my Mother."
- ✓ And again, kind of out of the blue, "I'm a fraud."
- ✓ He kept me pretty confused and doubting myself with his lies, stonewalling, smear campaign, etc. He presented to the world and to me initially as a very, very, very good man who was very devoted to me. It was a false persona. The 'marriage' lasted 4.5 years, and we were separated for most of it after the first year.
- ✓ I didn't know he had cross dressed for decades before our marriage and was doing porn, child porn and gay porn during our marriage (and who knows what else), until the last year or so. His pathological lying and lack of compassion bothered me even more than whether he is or isn't gay. I did stay embroiled in the mess far too long; he's a psychopath and knew how to 'hook' me.
- ✓ He shouted: "I don't do marriage!" in the middle of an argument about 2 years into our marriage. He was the one who pursued me and pushed me to get engaged to him. He was planning marriage for us way too early in the courtship (in retrospect, regrettably).

✓ He said about his ex wife, whom he constantly criticized, although I told him repeatedly I did not want to hear about her, "I felt like I was living with a man." I thought that was a weird thing to say, but gave him the benefit of the doubt at the time.

✓ He talked like he was homophobic, very critical of gay people; and he praised a particular minister for strongly speaking out against homosexuality, and for calling gays "queer."

✓ When we separated he told friends of ours that the separation was because he had had an affair, and that he took responsibility for it. He insinuated, and our friends concluded, that it was with a woman and it was a onetime thing. I filled them in on the truth: The reason we were separated was that he was a pathological liar, did porn including gay and child porn, cross dressed for decades before our marriage, that *he* left the marriage, he was an abuser, and he did not choose to change.

✓ During pre-marriage counseling, he announced to our minister and his wife, and to another couple present, that he intended not to bother me with sexual intimacy very much because of my delicate health. Yet, throughout our marriage he never bothered to help me physically unless it suited him and/or someone was watching that he wanted to impress, or he was trying to impress me. For example, he didn't bother to come home to help me when I returned from an out of town trip where I'd had to go to the ER for a severe stomach flu and I was still recovering. There are many other blatant examples of him neglecting to help me when I could have used the help.

✓ He constantly shouted at me in response to my bringing up a lie of his that I became aware of, "I don't lie *as much as you think I lie*!!!" He said the same thing about me to the minister and minister's wife we were 'counseling' with. (I was counseling; he was lying and playing games.)

✓ Before we married he courted my son hard, spending lots of time doing activities, hiking, shooting up rockets, etc., He spent more time with my son than with me. When we discussed separation, I asked him about his maintaining a relationship with my son, his stepson. (This was before I was aware of the child porn and gay porn.) He said about my son/his stepson, "He came with you; he goes with you." Then he told his family and others, and actually said to *me,* that *I* am keeping him from my son.

✓ He had told me that he had done porn in the past but did not do it anymore. When I found his computer had been to porn websites, I confronted him. I had a list of sites that his computer had been to that were obviously porn sites, but at that time I assumed that it was adult women he was looking at. First he denied it, and said, "There must be another explanation." (I guess he hadn't thought of another explanation yet.) A couple of days later he said, "I still do go to porn sites, but NOT THOSE SITES," referring to the sites I found on his computer. I had not discussed the specific sites with him. I had not checked them out, but he apparently thought I had or would. His comment was in the middle of an argument with a lot of back and forth. It didn't make sense, and at the time I overlooked it. Later, his words kept replaying in my mind, "NOT THOSE SITES," so I briefly (like 1/2 second) checked 2 of the sites on my list. One was gay men porn and the other was child (pre-pubescent girl) porn.

✓ Speaking of our marriage: "What got me into this mess was being horny."

✓ Numerous times when I pointed out problems to him, he accused me of 'scolding' him. I thought that sounded gay.

✓ "It must have been a brain seizure," referring to something he had done or said that I questioned him about. He used this one a few times.

From Jill

I was married 25 years to my gay ex-husband who is still quite adamant that he is not gay so the following comments or discussions we had were never open statements about being gay, but simply responses to my inquiries on certain situations:

✓ With regard to our infrequent sex – "it's like ice-cream. I don't want just boring vanilla."

✓ With regard to wearing thongs – "It's just a preference. There's nothing sexual about it."

✓ With regard to wearing a thong on the beach – "Less tan lines."

✓ With regard to looking at gay porn – "It's like a train wreck – you just have to stop and look. Just because I watch doesn't mean I want to go on a train that's about to crash."

✓ With regard to waxing ALL the hair off his body (including his genital area) – "The hair is irritating and pulls. It hurts when it pulls."

✓ And of course I was to believe there was absolutely NO connection between this extreme hair grooming and his searching for jobs on craigslist to be a nude model.

✓ With regard to looking at nude modeling jobs on craigslist – "LOL – I just think it's a hoot. I wouldn't do that."

✓ With regard to why he was taking Viagra when he was definitely not having sex with me – "I was just curious."

✓ With regard to why his guy 'friend' (who is openly gay) gave him a $400 coat for Christmas if they're just friends – "He's a very generous guy and he's got lots of money to spend."

✓ In response to receiving an ***Edible Arrangement*** from his guy 'friend' (who is openly gay), "I told him not to do anything."

✓ When questioned about why he was so tan all the time – "It's from shoveling snow."

✓ When questioned why he was looking on a website for exotic men's underwear, "You know I'm really particular about what underwear I wear. I was searching for the right kind."

✓ When questioned as to why ***cock sox*** was typed into the exotic men's underwear site, "They're comfortable."

✓ When questioned as to why he needed a ***dildo*** or a **plunger *handle*** up his butt during the few times he agreed to have sex, "I just like the anus stimulation – it's different."

✓ He told me that gay men hit on him but he had NO idea why!

From Sofia

✓ He hit the nail of his fat toe on the edge of the bed, later on in the evening I wanted to have sex. He replied angrily, "How can you be so inconsiderate and want to have sex after I just hit my fat toe???"

From Erin

✓ "Now that I'm dating a younger, prettier, more successful woman who likes my politics and music, I no longer desire to do the things I did when I was with you!"

From Louisa

✓ ***"It's your fault I had an affair because you didn't demonstrate enough that you loved me enough"***

Note the 'enough' – not that I didn't demonstrate my love, but that I didn't demonstrate it <u>enough</u>.

Other classics included:

✓ ***"X (name of lover) doesn't like me to be home late."***

This after 20 years of GEH rarely being home to eat with family or help with evening routine, he was suddenly able to be home before 6:00 pm because his gay lover wanted him around.

✓ ***"You're too tall so our children are too tall and that's why they are angry."***

I am 5'10" and the Gay Ex-Husband is 6'2". Our kids are 6'5", 6'3" and 6'1". Between us we have 8 brothers all well over 6' and 3 of our 4 parents are well over 6'. My 6'1" daughter has just this week bought herself a pair of shoes with 4" heels.

Somehow I don't think that being tall has ever bothered them, and that was certainly never the cause of their anger.

✓ *"All my friends think you are being unreasonable."*

I'm in stitches here .....

✓ *"Mum and I have been talking and together we have discovered that I am gay."*

You guessed it – no talking, no togetherness, no joint discovery.

✓ *"My lawyer agrees with me that your lawyer doesn't know what he is talking about."*

From Lisa

Things said...

✓ "You rely too much on Google, there is a lot of bad information out there" - as I've done a lot of research including your (Bonnie's) website and books.

✓ When I told him I wasn't all that into anal sex - his response "Well, I'm wired differently."

✓ When I asked him to go to a bisexual/married support group - his response: "My therapist and I discussed it and it is not necessary for me."

✓ He insists he is only bisexual, but really won't talk about it - hence, my need to do research. We are in the church.

✓ He insists he is only a "1" or "2" on the Kinsey scale.

✓ He was not interested in me, due to his low testosterone - of course, but I've been giving him his injections every two weeks for over a year now without any "reward."

✓ He is now overly concerned about his body and I get daily updates on his yoga, weight, waist size, and body fat.

✓ He tries on jeans and tells me which ones make his butt look good.

✓ He now wears bikini underwear (and gave me the explanation how men and their toilet habits work) - and apparently, Kohl's does not carry the type of underwear he needs.

✓ He does not like to go to the "gay" restaurant in town - but always wants to stop by South Beach in Miami.

✓ When shopping for clothes, he asked me how a shirt looked, and it was way too tight (he thought it looked good) - and my reaction was to go back to the clothes rack saying "let's get this gay over with." :-)

From Lil

Here is my ex-husband's story. You may have a similar one.

✓ The way I caught my gay husband was by checking his cell phone. I was never a wife who snooped, but I knew something was up. He was acting different and very distant. So one day he left his phone in our car, and I checked the numbers. One number popped out at me. I don't know why exactly, but it certainly did. It was a 312 area code which is a common area code in Chicago, but that number really hit me. I wrote it down and called it later. You will not be surprised that when I called I heard this greeting: "This is Man Phone, a great place to meet new hot exciting men." I will never forget those words.

So I watched his phone day after day. He called every day and sometimes numerous times. I was not sure how to confront him. When I finally did, he got very defensive and said he would leave. I said great. Hours later he came back and told me he did not want to go because he loved me and our three kids. He did not want a divorce and wanted to make it work. Then tearfully told me he was "fucked up" because as a teenager, he was abused by a priest. There you go-- his excuse.

I felt awful and researched what to do for him. I found out this abuse needed to be formally reported. So we went together to the Archdiocese of Chicago and made a formal report. It seems this particular priest was a habitual abuser which made me feel ever worse for him. The Archdiocese said we would both need help with this situation and they would pay for both of us to go into therapy. So we did.

They recommended a clinical psychologist, whom I thought was great, but it was not so. My husband and I saw her every week for two years, each of us individually and also once a week as a couple. It did at the time seem to be working. He was somewhat more attentive, but the therapist was trying her best to convince me that he loved me and was working hard to save our marriage. She would say to me, "What is it that you want? You have a man who loves you and your kids and wants this to work."

I was not buying it completely. He seemed to be working at it, although I was not so sure he was not gay. In fact our couple sessions usually were scheduled right after his appointments, and I kept thinking each time we would go that this would be the appointment that he would give me the truth. It never happened. Instead, the therapy turned it all around by acting as if I had some sort of issue. Why was I not getting that my husband had issues from childhood abuse? He was not gay, and loved me.

We continued therapy through the two years. One day, we had an argument, and he said that he wanted a divorce. I went at him for the real reason for this and finally there were the words I had waited for. "I am gay, Lil." The truth was only told at this point because it was good for him. His father, a very opinionated, old-fashioned man who he was afraid of, had just gone into a coma that he was not coming out of, so he felt this was a safe, perfect time for him.

So to sum it up, my con man ex-husband even conned the therapist. Unbelievable, still today. And by the way, I do believe he was abused which is unforgivable, but if this makes any sense, I believe his abuse was somewhat consensual. He was a young man and minor so that makes it so wrong, but in putting pieces of this puzzle together, I am sure my husband knew exactly what was going on with this priest. He had a friend being abused and used to see him come and go from the rectory. So I truly believe my ex put himself in that situation. Not that it makes it right one bit.

From Mari

Some of my husband's quotes:

- ✓ I hate you because you remind me of my mother.
- ✓ I will not be able to have sex with any other women because you said that and I believed.
- ✓ You are unattractive.
- ✓ You must be the most frustrated person of all since you spent many years of your life trying to help me and you failed.
- ✓ You destroyed our family.
- ✓ I am not attracted to you because you are not feminine.
- ✓ There are nights that I want to push you out of the bed. You make me feel nauseated.

From Lynn

✓ Despite contracting AIDS, herpes, and rectal cancer from living a reckless homosexual lifestyle for 20+ years, my husband says he is not gay. He did it rather than cheat on me with a woman because that would be an emotional relationship.

From Kate

Bonnie, you have been a great help to me over the last 3 years. Mine couldn't argue with the evidence as I found videos on his laptop dated back over a decade of him having group sex with men but he still had a go!!!

- ✓ "I'm not gay; it's just you are so bad in bed and because I am such a loyal honorable person that I sleep with men out of respect to you."

- ✓ After finding genital crabs 2 weeks after giving birth to our first child, he arrived with a very slick explanation of a swimming costume I had tried on week before at a shop (which was true) and told me how lucky I was that I had such a trusting husband to believe this. Otherwise I would have had serious explaining to do on what I might have been doing whilst pregnant or in the maternity ward!

- ✓ I was with him all my life since being 18, and he still has been my only partner. I had a lot of abuse, and the best sex was having a pillow put over my head because I was so ugly.

- ✓ Now 38 and enjoying being on my own with my 3 kids, I have a good psychotherapist and I'm building my career back up. I found the radio shows a lifeline from the UK.

- ✓ To other women, I am intelligent and well educated. I am finally able to say that after years of being told by him that I am just not one of life's copers and only capable of doing a Mickey Mouse job. I now work as a family doctor and am being promoted to teach other doctors, but I still believed a lot of the rubbish he said because like other abused spouses, I was so isolated throughout the marriage. He wouldn't even let me go for food shopping. There was no-one to counteract the continuous negative feed and domestic abuse!

I had a lot of the other comments made to other women that I have heard on radio show over last 3 years, and I hope you continue your work. I still get comfort every day from your simple " if he likes a penis, he's gay" approach, and the time you ran through 10 things gay husbands like to say to avoid sex!!

From Liz

✓ All that sex is only in the movies or television.

✓ I don't have to date; I am married.

✓ We will have a relationship after the kids leave home.

✓ Get a life.

✓ You act like you are starving.

From Susanne

- ✓ "How can I be gay?...Look at all these tattoos." (Naked female bodies; heart with my name in it)
- ✓ "How can I be gay? I own guns."

From Allison

✓ When my ex husband finally admitted the truth about what he had been up to all those years he said to me, "I can't believe you didn't know!"

Like somehow I was the one at fault! He had spent years letting me think our problems were all my fault so I guess he didn't know how to behave otherwise. When I tell people what he said, they are speechless!

From Claire

✓ My husband used to frequent public toilets (and other gay venues) on a regular basis for sex – yuuuuuk. I used to feel nauseated for many months just thinking about it. And because it was close to where we lived-- I still live in the area--I am still driving past these public toilets on a daily basis! Thankfully, the nausea has stopped with some training and ability to now drive past without looking at how many cars are parked outside the toilets. It gets very busy during peak hours!

His explanation:

✓ "I don't know why I used to do it. I must have been in a dissociative state when it happened." He is a Manager of a large mental health service and a Family Therapist! Go figure.

One more gem:

✓ "It could have been much worse you know. I could have become emotionally involved. At least I was true to you in that way."

My response:

✓ "I wish you had become emotionally involved and found some true intimacy with someone you loved authentically and our marriage would have ended sooner perhaps and not 28 years down the track!"

From Michelle

Here is a darnedest thing the GID would often say when I approach the subject of sex.

✓ It would take his internal energy to have sex with me and since he needed that energy to train, we wouldn't be able to have sex.

When I say "train," I mean he is a mixed martial arts instructor (yep, cage fighter).

From Lynn

✓ He told me he knows now he wants "the tenderness of a woman, to hold a woman's hand, to go out with a woman, but blow jobs from a man." But is not gay!!!!!!

I hope he finds someone who would put up with that. I just hope he doesn't ruin some other women's life like he did mine for 25 years.

From Karen

✓ Here is a Quote that my ex-husband used to try to tell me to explain he was not gay and that what he did was "normal" after being involved in homosexual porn, meeting up with men supposedly just to masturbate, and being arrested at a park for meeting up with men:

"Karen, there have been numerous studies done showing the attraction of men to penises." I said, "Only if you're gay!!" He looked at me with an irritated expression. He wanted me to stay married to him! What nerve!

From Jenny

✓ When asked about the day I caught him at work in an office cubicle having some kind of touching going on with a co-worker who was in his mid 30s and had NEVER had a girlfriend and with whom he had shared a hotel bed with on a trip:

1) "I don't remember."

2) "You must have imagined it."

By the look on their faces and the erection that he had, I'm sure he'll never forget it or at least I won't!

✓ When trying to solve the problem why he could not have sex with me anymore:

"So all you care about in this marriage is my sexual performance?"

Wouldn't any wife wonder why their husband could not be stimulated by her, but he could masturbate just fine by himself in the shower?

✓ When asked why after 23 years of regular sex he was suddenly interested in anal sex:

"I just wanted to try something new."

From Monica

✓ In response to my questions about why our marriage has no physical or emotional intimacy and how can we change that, I was told, "Two years ago, right after our daughter was born, I asked you if you could lose a lot of weight and get really skinny. You ignored that. You even told me when I brought it up again that that question made you mad. So that's why there is no intimacy."

✓ And the best one: "There will be no intimacy in our marriage until you sign the postnuptial agreement I emailed you."

✓ In response to my *sincerely and kindly and still at that time hopefully offered* suggestion for his upcoming physical exam that he maybe ask to have his testosterone level checked, "There is nothing physically wrong with me."

✓ After I pretty much forced him to go see a therapist to find out what is blocking him from wanting to be physically or emotionally intimate with me, he came back and reported, "He says it is clear to him that I am angry with you, and he said anger prevents intimacy." He never went back again to find out how to stop being angry or even why he is angry; it just became a good justification for continued avoidance of intimacy.

From Julie

✓ My husband would say, "You should have been a nun, because you love God so much, and you don't really need a man. God's enough for you." I had no choice; I didn't have a man who loved me or wanted to make love with me.

✓ I did love God and knew he loved me, so I became more religious. My husband only condemned the God I believed in; he didn't understand. The only way I could make sense out of my fate was to seek others with something in common and devote myself to God all the more.

✓ My husband tossed me out and told me I was worth nothing, useless, and a waste of food. God said everyone had value. Only God could get me through and I knew it.

✓ I became a secular religious in an integrated community, where you can live a more devoted life while being married. It gave purpose to my life meaning, all of which my husband had robbed from me. I'm still part of the community, but my gay husband has died. I could remarry, but I haven't been able to have luck in the dates for my type and I understand nothing about what real men are like. I carry the scars within …even still.

✓ When I found out my husband had invited a man to live with him in the house while I was on vacation, he said, "I was just helping this poor fellow out because he is homeless."

✓ When I asked my husband why he married a woman when he wasn't attracted to women, he said, "I wanted a breeder, nothing more." I was only a breeder to him.

✓ When I asked my husband when he was planning on telling me the truth about his hidden life, he said he just couldn't find the right time. When I said early on when I still had my youth would of been a good time so then I could of found someone else, he said, "Well I needed you to watch the kids and show up at business dinners because it looked good for the business to have a nice family.

✓ When I was upset over the fact he had invited a man to live with him while I was on vacation, and he finally couldn't convince me that it was a homeless fellow he was helping out, he said, "Why are you upset? I've been seeing him for 15 years." When I questioned if that makes it right, he then said, "It's okay. It's nothing new--you're over reacting. We had been married 24 years to date. When I started crying, he said, "Don't be a baby. It's not that bad. I only slept with a man, not another woman," as if that made it okay.

✓ When I said, "Man or woman--it's still sex outside of the marriage; it's still infidelity," then he said, "You're homophobic!" I said, No, I'm married!"

✓ There's a difference. I have a right to be upset we are married. He kept screaming about his rights. Then I said, "What about my rights? What about my needs for love? He then told me that I don't understand that he has stronger needs than me. He said gay men have stronger sexual needs than heterosexual women.

From Cindy

✓ I remember traveling in his car and he went into the filling station to pay for gas. I had dropped something on the floor and reached down to pick it up. Under the seat were two PLAYGIRL magazines. When he got back into the car, I asked him about the magazines. He told me he had bought them for me. Holy smoke! They were three months old!! Did he forget to give them to me?

✓ He told our grown children that this new friend and him met at a bookstore. They just happened to be in the same aisle and began talking about the same book. My ex was 57 and his new "hubby" (yes, they were married in NY) was only 28. Can't seem to have the same interest! They then went and had coffee together at Borders and thus the relationship began. My children call Borders "Homewreckers.com." When I confronted my ex about this, he said, "Don't you ever stir up a conversation with ladies at Joann's or Michaels about yarn or fabric?" My reply was, "Yes, but I don't take them home and sleep with them." That night was not pretty.

From Erin

✓ My ex once told me, "All men are like me (about sleeping with other men) and that it wasn't public knowledge to women because it was a "man thing!" OMG! He is still in deep, deep, denial but now with another wife and 9 month old daughter: So sad!

From Jennifer

- ✓ GAY #1 (my ex-husband of 10 years): Upon my query of, "Where do you go when you leave the house every weekend for the past 10 years at 5:00 am?"

  His response: "Walmart."

  FYI - He never came home with anything from Walmart.

- ✓ GAY#2 (my ex significant other of 7 years): Upon my discovery of an email from a secret email account sent by him to another woman's' husband from Craigslist propositioning him to meet him in the woods and perform oral sex on him:

  His Response: "I'm not gay - I just like to have sex with men."

  FYI - He's still sticking to that story.

From Sienna

✓ The most glaring evidence to me that my husband was gay, in hindsight of course, was the anal sex issue. He constantly pushed me to allow him to penetrate me anally, and even at one point asked me to wear a strap-on and penetrate him anally. I was completely shocked and repulsed by this.

He claimed, however, that many straight people enjoyed this. I was not kinky enough. He even showed me a magazine article that claimed this was a great way to spice up married sex. So it was hard for me to accept that there was anything wrong with it.

I do not believe that him wanting to have anal sex meant he was gay, but I do believe his growing obsession with anal sex was a sign. He reached a point where that was all he wanted from me and all he would talk about. Eventually, he would not have sex with me at all unless it was anal sex.

✓ When we tried anything else he could not keep an erection, and of course he blamed it on me saying I wasn't attractive, wasn't doing it right (whatever act I was performing on him), and other excuses that made me the problem and not him.

✓ In addition to that, after refusing him over and over again, I found an anal balloon pump (at least I think that's what it was called) hidden in our bathroom. His excuse, of course, was that he was not gay. He just really wanted to try anal sex and because I would not consent to that, (of course it was my fault) he had to fulfill those desires on his own.

✓ He always said, "You are just too vanilla (not kinky) and I have desires you won't fulfill, so I choose to fulfill them myself. Those desires don't mean I'm gay, lots of straight men enjoy anal stimulation." As if that were not enough, I also found a large "toy" penis hidden in the house at one point. I don't know what to call it other than a "toy" because I'm not sure what anyone would do with a thing like that. I never told him that I found it, because it was too painful for me and at that point I was pretty sure he was gay anyway.

✓ Another red flag was that we both had Hotmail email accounts, and several times I would go on the computer and find a website called hot male (dot)com in the history. I clicked on it and was mortified to find that it was gay porn. His excuse? "I misspelled the web address." I am pretty sure the creators of this site had that excuse in mind when coming up with that name! The first time it happened, I brushed it off, though I was very disturbed by what I had seen.

✓ This was when I began checking his computer more frequently, and also when he started clearing his history every time and using his iPhone more than the computer. I found similar things on his phone, then he put a passcode lock on his iPhone. When I asked why he said, "I am entitled to a little privacy." Well, there is a big difference between privacy and secrecy!

✓ One thing that sticks out to me as I look back was the night he disappeared and I could not find him anywhere. He was gone all night and I had called his cell phone dozens of times and even called the local police and hospitals to see if he had been in a wreck or maybe even arrested. His excuse was "I was so tired after work that after I went into Walmart to get a few things we needed, and I decided to just sit a moment and rest in my car. I must have fallen asleep." Our home was right down the street! What trouble would it have been to come home and get in the bed? I don't have any proof of what actually happened that night, but the excuse sounded so ridiculous that I really feel that he was with someone that night.

✓ Something else I remember is that he would do my hair and makeup for me when we were going out and even pick out what I wore. I was shocked at how tasteful his opinion on clothes was and how much better I looked when I let him dress me and do my hair and makeup!

✓ I laughed at this at first, and he always said it was because he grew up in a family of all women so he was taught a lot about such things. I accepted this excuse, but as time went on it began to get very weird. My girlfriends would say, "Oh I love your hairdo, who did your hair?" When I would say, "My husband did," an awkward silence would follow. I guess my dear friends didn't have the heart to tell me what they already knew.

From Glynis

✓ "Why do you talk about sex all the time?"

✓ One time on a married couple's retreat I told him I felt bad because all the other young women were talking about how their husbands always wanted sex. Mine responded, "Well, think about how I feel listening to the guys talk about their high sex drives."

✓ "I'm not like other men."

✓ "I get turned on my touch, not sight."

✓ "I don't know what's wrong with me."

✓ "It's never enough for you!"

✓ While about to have sex one night he said to me, "You gotta help me you know." (get him aroused)

✓ I said "I wish you were more sexually attracted to me." He responded, "It's not you." (this one he's said many times)

✓ He wouldn't want to make love if our teenage girls were still awake because "he wasn't raised that way." (We had a lock on our door)

✓ I told him I'd love to make love to him all night long (figure of speech of course) he said according to a book he read "that only happens in the movies."

✓ "You're smothering me." (of course it was always said with a laugh)

✓ One night recently he wanted to make love. I told him I wasn't feeling well. (I have no interest now) and he said, "Okay, but we still need to pray cause that's the most important thing. It was no problem for him!

From Mary Beth

✓ "It's your fault for telling me about what you found on Craigslist. That's the reason I went on there," after catching my ex in a full day conversation with a man he was hoping to meet up with later in the week for oral sex. I had discovered CL after placing an ad to find a home for our pet rabbit and stumbled across "personals."

✓ "All men do this; it's normal." I believed him for a while, until I met Bonnie.

✓ "It was only a conversation; I did NOTHING. I had no intention of meeting with him. Look at my calendar and my busy schedule for the day I was planning to meet him." Well, then why would you do this to someone? Why would you make arrangements and talk about oral sex if you had no intention of meeting up with him?

✓ "You're the one that left ME! That's what I did during our break up." After finding explicit instant message conversations with a boy/man after I returned to make our marriage work.

✓ "All is okay now. I talked to our marriage counselor once by myself and I have it all figured out. I will not do this again. I am straight." It was a phase he was going through when I left him and all is good because he talked to marriage counselor.

✓ "I went to Shampoo (gay bar) with a bunch of people for a birthday party." I don't even know what to say about that.

From Rachel

✓ When I found his stash of transsexual porn:

"It's just a fetish. I don't pay attention to the penis; I just like the feminine form."

✓ When I found his online dating profiles of straight men looking for transsexuals and gays: "I don't look at them as men. If it looks like a woman, it's a woman, and it's just an online thing anyways. I'd never actually do it."

✓ When I found out he'd been frequenting transsexual prostitutes:

"Well, you said that one time when we were 19 and drunk that you'd be okay with it if it was a guy, so you kind of gave me permission. So don't bitch about it - this is kind of your fault, too." This was funny, because wait, I thought you didn't look at trannys as guys! If you pay attention, they'll always trip themselves up!

✓ When I asked him if he was gay:

"No ... maybe I'm a little bisexual, but I'm NOT attracted to men. Who cares; it's who I am. I'm not ashamed of it." Then why is it such a huge freaking secret? Afterwards, he denied he has ever said it.

✓ When I told him that one day he's not going to be able to find a transsexual, and going to do it with an "actual" man: "I'm not attracted to men. Eww, they're so hairy and gross. Never." Still at this point he's denying he said he's bisexual, and he denies he's gay as well.

✓ When he left his email up accidentally and I found out he'd been meeting GUYS on the internet, not transsexuals, and having anonymous sex A LOT:

"It was only a few times. No, I'm not attracted to men at all. How dare you go into my private email, you bitch!"

Still at this point he's denying he said he's bisexual, and he denies he's gay as well.

From Robbie

- ✓ When I asked him why he had shaved his genital area, he said, "I did it for you." (We had never done this sort of thing before, and I was very surprised by it).

- ✓ "I want my own friends that you don't have to know about."

- ✓ When I found photos of transvestites and male pornography on the computer: "I don't know how it got there. Probably a hacker." ROFL. Kind of funny when I think about it now.

- ✓ When the transvestite guy came up to him in a parking lot while we were shopping, pointed at me, and asked if I was pregnant, he said, "I don't know who that was! You're just paranoid!"

- ✓ When I found he had posted on a transvestite membership meet up site and confronted him about it: "I was doing research for a book!"

From Carol

✓ I once suspected that he was having an affair.
He assured me that I was the "only woman in his life."

From Maggie

✓ When I confronted my husband, it was accompanied by a letter from my attorney stating I wanted to pursue a divorce action because of his numerous homosexual affairs. The attorney had told me, however, NOT to show him any of the evidence I had and not to engage in arguments with him. So when he asked me one day, "What affairs?" it was difficult to just shrug and walk away. He commented several times that I was just crazy.

✓ He found out the answer at mediation when my attorney presented a laundry list of his indiscretions including names, addresses, and telephone numbers.

I guess he also found out who was crazy and who wasn't.

From Carol

✓ "I think there are degrees of gayness(?)...and I'm not all gay...just somewhat gay" This coming from a guy who spent the last 10 years going to Cuba to have sex with young black men, still watches gay porn on the internet, and hasn't been intimate with his straight wife in over 15 years.

✓ "They (his Black boy toys) were really just friends" ....with benefits I assume.

✓ Oh, and here's a dilly. "I wasn't with them all the time..I really just went there to enjoy the unique Cuban culture." It was unique alright.

✓ I confronted him about his email love note to one of his playthings, and he responded, "I think of you all the time my love (mi amor) and want to make love with you again." His response came out of his lying mouth, "I don't love anybody there...that's just gay parlance, Carol."

✓ And are you ready for this..."I'm just different...I like to think of it as broadening my horizons." And when I retorted with a nasty comment, then it was, "I'm just joking Carol. Where has your sense of humor gone?" What an A-hole he can be.

✓ And this one takes first prize I think...."It's not really like cheating when it's with another man...if it was with another woman...then you might feel like you had to compete or something...but you shouldn't see it as cheating when it's a man." WTF IS THAT!!!! Please forgive my language!

And he is so deceptive....I know he is keeping in touch with his boy toy occasionally, but he lies so convincingly with, "I haven't heard from him or anyone there in nearly a year." This is mainly because I've been able to block most of the emails! But I just read one from a lady whom he rented a room from there, and she was very complicit with his gay crap saying she had the "amigo" over to see if there was a message from my gay husband. I deleted it of course.

From Joanne

✓ "He is a friend from childhood... we grew up together."

From Robin

- ✓ My ex said that the reason he was looking at gay websites was that he was depressed and that he couldn't talk to me because I never listened to him.

- ✓ He said that it wasn't the gay websites he was looking at that caused our marriage to fail, it was me not being supportive of him. (WOW)

- ✓ He also said that his looking at gay porn was just his way of dealing with his depression, everyone deals with depression in their own way. (Oh brother!)

From Chris

✓ One Friday evening, I tried to initiate sex and he said, "But--We just did that, Tuesday!"

✓ While I was about three months pregnant with our first child, I tried to initiate sex and he said, "But--the baby will see!"

✓ "I should have married a nice, Jewish girl. They lose interest in sex as soon as they get the ring on."

✓ "You have to understand: you and I will never be as close as I am to my male friends. It's just the way things are. Men and women can never really understand each other and be friends." (I have often wondered if they were having sex at the time, as we were engaged, and the other guy was also engaged, and neither couple was having sex because Sex Before Marriage Is Wrong.)

Final Thoughts

from

Bonnie Kaye

I would like to leave you with two additional pieces from my newsletters. I hope they tie up the loose ends for you!

GAYLIGHTING April 2010

In our support chats, hardly a week goes by where someone doesn't bring up the term, "Gas Lighting." This is a term taken from the old movie Gas Light from 1944 staring Ingrid Bergman and Charles Boyer. Although I never saw the movie until a few weeks ago, I was certainly familiar with the terminology from members of our support group who used it frequently to describe their situations with their gay spouses. After watching it, I realized that this terminology certainly has a connection for many of us.

According to the Internet:

From the film's title, "gaslighting" acquired the meaning of ruthlessly manipulating an individual, for nefarious reasons, into believing something other than the truth.

Well, that certainly sums it up for some of us, doesn't it? I know that I was made to feel "crazy" if I suggested to my husband that maybe...just maybe...he's.... ummmmm... oh yes—"bisexual." That was the nice way for me to frame it in my own mind back in those days. He would tell me I'm out of my mind and...oh yes...CRAZY. How could I ever think something so horrible and disgusting? Now in the beginning, I felt a big sense of relief. But as time wore on, the relief turned to doubt— and not doubt about HIM—but rather about ME! And once self-doubt starts, it's a quick progression down that road called "I can't trust my judgment anymore." Like the peeling onion, your self-confidence gets peeled down one layer at a time until it shrinks to nothing.

The problem with too many gay husbands is that they have to find a way to protect the lie they are living. Those three little words—and I don't mean "I love you" but rather "I AM GAY"--are too difficult to say to you—and often to themselves. For them, it is easier to just make you think you are CRAZY when questioning their repeated lies that start to pile up and make little if any sense. How many times have you heard, "Are you out of your mind?" "How could you think such a thing?" or "What are you—CRAZY?" With a gay husband, in almost all of our cases we've heard these words more than once or twice.

So now I've added a new word to my "**Bonnie Kaye's Pocket Dictionary of Gay Husband Lingo**" which includes some of those clarifying terms that I've made famous like Limbo Men and Straight-Gay Men. Now I am adding the term **GAYLIGHTING**.

Definition: "Your husband's attempts to make you think that you are losing your mind when in fact you are just finding out his truth."

Trust me—you're not crazy, you're just being "**gaylighted**."

NEW EPIPHANY
GAY MEN DON'T THINK STRAIGHT
July 2013

Every few years, an epiphany hits me like a ton of bricks. The first one was in 2001 when I realized that we became women who we were not necessarily supposed to become because our husbands are gay. Instead of working to grow emotionally and professionally, we are spiritually muted or stagnated for years living in a state of what I call "Muck"...much like sinking in quicksand. That is because we dance in that "circle of crazy" which means running around in circles like a dog chasing after its tail. Even the dog is in better shape than we are because sometimes he gets a hold of his tail--we just keep sinking further into helplessness.

Several epiphanies later, I now have a new one. This comes from 30 years and over 90,000 women asking me dozens of different questions that usually start the same way:

"HOW COULD HE DO THIS TO ME?"

It's very simple--**he's GAY**.

And here's my newest epiphany:

"GAY MEN DON'T THINK STRAIGHT."

Please don't misunderstand me. This is not a put down on gay people at all. It's just a reality based on

85

years of observation. I am the first to say that I don't think gay. That is because **I am straight**. Once again--an observation.

So when women ask me how their gay husbands can do the things they do, it's quite simple--they are **GAY. They don't belong in a marriage to you. PERIOD.**

The problem with our women is that they keep expecting their husbands to act as if they *are straight-- not gay*. You forget that gay men who complain about their unhappiness are unhappy because they are married to you--a woman. And even though your husband was for the most part all excited about the "opportunity" to marry you before you said, "I do," he was saying, "I hope I can, I hope I can make love to her, I hope she'll believe me when I pretend to be straight, I hope I won't keep fantasizing about men anymore, I hope those things I've done with guys will be in the past, I hope that if I can't resist these urges and she finds out, she won't leave me," etc. etc. You see, while you were entering the marriage filled with hopes and dreams, he was entering your marriage filled with the hope that he could "pull it off."

Don't ever believe that your gay husband just found out he was gay after he married you--after 10, 20, 30, or 40 years. That isn't true. And don't believe that he thought all men--including straight men--fantasize about being with men or have occasional sexual encounters with men because that is NOT true. And he knows it isn't true--he is just justifying his sexual fantasies and encounters. And why? **He doesn't want to be gay.**

I do believe that most gay men marry you because they love you--but let me clarify that by saying that they love you to *the best of their ability as gay men*. They love you the way they would love a sister or a cousin--but you are not his family--you are his **WIFE**. And as a wife, you are expecting more out your husband than to love you as a family member or best friend. That's where the disconnect begins. Some of us have that happen sooner than later in a marriage--but eventually, it does happen. And when things are not heating up in the bedroom, that's where the anger, resentment, and blame begin.

You: Why does it feel like I have to ask for sex all of the time?

Him: Why are you always thinking about sex?

You: Other women spend romantic evenings with their husbands.

Him: You are watching too many movies. It doesn't happen that way in real life.

You: We've only been married a couple of years. Why don't you make love to me?

Him: What are you? A nymphomanic? All you think about is sex, sex, sex.

Here is the disconnect. As a gay man, he is also thinking about sex, sex, sex. But he is not thinking about having it with you. When he thinks about sex with you, he is thinking about a *way out of having sex* with you. Just like the thought of having sex with your brother or uncle would be repulsive to you, he has the same thought when it comes to you. It's not that he doesn't love you--he just doesn't love you the way you love him--**because he is gay**. He can love you, but he can't be "in love" with you. **He is gay--he doesn't know how.**

Gay men in denial who have a deep enough desire to stay married because they can't face living in a "gay world" will go through the motions. They can talk the talk. After all, they've been practicing their whole lives observing straight people. They can walk the walk--they know what a "straight walk" looks like. But they can't do the "dirty" indefinitely no matter how hard they try. And after a while, it becomes "dirty" to them. It becomes as incestuous to them as it would be for us to have sex with a family member--or even your best girlfriend whom you love--but not as a lover.

Why do we keep expecting gay men to be straight men? That is the faulty thinking that **we** *have*. Every response they have with you is based on their gay thinking--not on straight thinking. The resentment they have towards you is because you are a woman who wants them to be a straight man. Why wouldn't you? He married you. He promised to love you through everything--but he didn't understand that everything meant being a husband who wants intimacy and sex with his wife as part of the marital deal.

When your husband married you, he figured he could do it and maybe enjoy it. After all, he could always close his eyes and fantasize about his dream man. Many of these gay husbands do just that--and they have told me so. But they don't want to do more than they have to do to convince you that they are straight. After all, if they can get an erection every now and then--even if they can't keep it during your intimate moments--that will prove to you that they are straight. And if they lose the erection in the middle of one of those moments--no problem. It's your fault, isn't it? If he can get one, he takes the credit, but can't keep it going, then you get the credit because it must be your fault. Let's see, you're too fat...thin...dirty...smelly...flat chested....big chested...have bad breath...breathe too loud...demand too much...boring during sex...didn't clean the house enough, don't use the right shampoo, etc., etc., etc.

And then you ask me how they could do this to you.

So ladies, here's where my new epiphany should become your new mantra:

GAY MEN DON'T THINK STRAIGHT BECAUSE THEY ARE GAY!

You need to say this over and over again to yourself daily whether you are still in your marriage or not. You see, we keep wondering how they can worse after they leave the marriage. We keep thinking like straight women who have a straight husband:

Us: Maybe now that he has left, he'll realize how much he has hurt me.

Them: I gave up so much of my life for her. I was such a good husband and provider. I gave her everything I had, and all she did was complain and complain about sex. She's so ungrateful.

Yes, we just **don't get it**. Women have come to me and said, "He's willing to give up his family for a roll in the hay with someone? Sex means more to him than his family?

Yes, **you just don't get it.** It's not about sex--it's about being gay and being free of living a lie where he can never please you. It's about him feeling the kind of love and excitement with a man that he can never feel for you because he is gay. And say it again:

GAY MEN DON'T THINK STRAIGHT
BECAUSE THEY ARE GAY.

The key to healing from this nightmare is to realize that you can't do anything about it other than accept it. You can't personalize it. When your husband or ex-husband blames you for his unhappiness, you can believe it because you are a woman. You can never be the wife he needs because he doesn't need a wife--he needs a man. He is gay.

When he blames you for ANYTHING, hold your head high because you need to believe this has NOTHING to do with you. You didn't create it, and you can't change it. In Bonnie Kaye terms that means: You didn't break him--you can't fix him. Stop trying.

Nothing upsets me more than women who tell me that some of the problems in the marriage happened because of their behavior so they have to take some of the blame. Well sister, here's the news--you don't have to take any of the blame. You married someone who can never make you feel good about yourself because he was rejecting you on some level since the day he married you. Even though he didn't want to hurt you, he couldn't help himself because he is gay.

What does that mean? He resented you. You became the enemy. You were the keeper of his internal prison he created, and **YOU** held the key that you refused to hand him to escape. It doesn't matter that *he* wanted to marry you, nor does it matter that he refuses to leave his safety net and comfort level of leading a "straight life." Now you are the one who "keeps him trapped" into being someone he doesn't really want to be---namely your husband..

This is where another *disconnect* sets in. He continually picks, picks, picks--and he is picking at you and on you because of his frustration. He'll look to blame you for the problems in the marriage. After all, he's done everything to make you happy, but you are never happy. He's a good provider. He's a good father. What's the problem in the marriage? It has to be YOU. In his mind, he does what he believes is the right thing to do--other than giving you sex every time you ask for it--and don't you keep asking? What is with you?

Since most of these men don't or won't tell you the truth *until they are ready--and sadly, too many will never be ready, even when they leave you--*you slowly begin the deterioration process that strips down your self-esteem one layer at a time. You lose your footing because no matter how hard you try, your husband doesn't love you the way you know a man should love a woman. You're not stupid--but you sure are feeling very stupid because nothing you do is making your husband happy. When you don't know why all of your efforts don't bear the results you want, you finally understand what is wrong in your relationship--**YOU ARE INADEQUATE**. You have made every attempt to make your husband love you by showing him with love, affection, and passion--but nothing helps. What is wrong with you?

This is where the anger, depression, and worthless-ness starts taking over your psyche. Many of our gay husbands/ex husbands are passive-aggressive. They use a "slap and smile" strategy meaning they slap you down (mostly emotionally, but in some cases physically) and then tell you that they love you. Our "perception" of love gets distorted. As long as you hear those words "I love you," you feel there is a chance if only you can change some of your ways. You know what upsets him most--**SEX**. Other than that, he's not "that bad." As your family and friends keep telling you, "He's a good dad. He's a good provider. You go on nice vacations. He's not a

WOMANIZER. You are a lucky woman." **Message: There's nothing wrong with him. You should be happy.**

So why aren't you? You start feeling guilty because you think you don't have the right to complain. Then you start reading magazine articles that say most relationships "lose their groove" sexually in time, but the friendship and love is still there. As the song goes, "Don't worry--be happy." Right? *Wrong.*

This is not about straight couples who get caught up with life on life's terms over the years where sex can diminish due to health issues or job pressures. This is about a gay man who has never made you feel valued as a woman--only as a sexual aggressor who has turned him off. It's about losing confidence in everything you do because no matter how much you have done, nothing is working. So many of our women try transforming themselves by going through life-changing surgery like gastric bypasses, breast implants, liposuction, and plastic surgery in order to make themselves more beautiful so their husbands will desire them. That's because he usually throws in those little excuses, "If only you weren't so heavy....if only you would lose weight...if only your breasts weren't so small....if only your body wasn't so flabby....if only, if only, if only.

Ha, ha, ha. Like changing this will make their husbands want them sexually more. They soon find out that "enhancing your appearance" to make yourself more beautiful is an act in futility. Your husband doesn't want you more beautiful--he wants a man--he is gay.

When you are a normal woman, years of getting the message that you are 'abnormal" deprives you of ever knowing who you really are. There won't be much personal growth or actualizing here because you are too busy trying to get your husband to love you which means "desire you." You have to learn to accept the **way you want your husband to love you WILL NEVER HAPPEN BECAUSE HE IS A GAY MAN!**

Never mistake "cuddling with you" for "passion" with you. If it gives you some false illusion that "cuddling" means loving you, then you are deluding yourself. A marriage doesn't need cuddling as its primary source of affection. It needs the passion and desire that that makes you feel like you can climb a mountain or float on a cloud. A straight man will never just "do it" to make you happy. He will make you happy because it makes him happy when you are sexually satisfied. He loves to touch you. Cuddling is secondary--not the primary reason he wants to touch you. When a man loves you, he wants to "make love" to you.

I have been with my boyfriend for 19 years and 6 months. We have a beautiful and regular sex life that is always top of the line even at our age. As he explains to me, "Making love to you is the best way for me to express how much I love you." Yep, that is how a straight man thinks. We are both so in synch with each other because we know what pleases each other. After nearly two decades, I can tell you that he still works just as hard to please me because to him IT IS NOT WORK. It's passion that has built our intimacy to survive those difficult time when sex isn't possible due to medical issues. The medical issues are never an excuse--they are just a delay knowing things will be better and we will be fine. That's the difference between a straight man and a gay man. Straight men want sex with you because you are a woman--gay men don't want sex with you because you are a woman.

In closing, repeat these words every day:

GAY MEN DON'T THINK STRAIGHT

GAY MEN DON'T THINK STRAIGHT

You'll know you finally understand this when you stop hurting over something you have no control over. Stop personalizing it for the sake of your own mental health. Distance yourself emotionally so that one day you can truly heal. Don't continue to let his homosexuality define who you are. Remember--you are straight and he is gay.

BONNIE KAYE'S
STRAIGHT WIVES CLUB
<u>ON-GOING SUPPORT</u>

No woman ever has to feel like she is isolated and alone anymore. I offer the following support:

1. Online support chat in the U.S. and Canada three times a week

2. Online support for the United Kingdom and Europe once a week

3. Online support for adult children of gay fathers once a week

4. Painpals for any woman who needs to connect one-on-one with others

5. Monthly newsletters to help validate your feelings moving ahead

6. Weekly Sunday night radio show on line

7. Books that can be bought at:

www.BonnieKayeBooks.com

8. Healing weekends to meet other women in person twice a year--one in September in Philadelphia and the other in March in Houston

About the Author

Bonnie Kaye is an internationally recognized relationship counselor/author in the field of straight/gay marriages. She has provided relationship counseling and support for nearly 30 years to more than 85,000 women who have sexually dysfunctional husbands due to homosexuality, bisexuality, or other sexual addictions and fetishes. She is considered an authority in this field by other professionals and the media. Kaye has published eight books on straight/gay relationships, which have sold thousands of copies. Her website **www.Gayhusbands.com** has consistently remained in the number one position on Google, Yahoo, and other major search engines since its launching in the year 2000. When media contacts want an expert, they go to Bonnie Kaye who has more experience and expertise than any other person in the United States. Her official book website is located at **www.BonnieKayeBooks.com**. Kaye's support network has over 7,000 women around the world who receive her free monthly newsletter. She also has online computer support chat as well as a weekly internet radio show on Sundays, *Straight Wives Talk Show* on www.Blogtalkradio.com that can be accessed 24/7 around the world via the computer.

Kaye's other books include: *The Gay Husband Checklist for Women Who Wonder; Straight Wives: Shattered Lives (Volumes 1 and 2); ManReaders: A Woman's Guide to Dysfunctional Men; Bonnie Kaye's Straight Talk; How I Made My Husband Gay: Myths About Straight Wives; Doomed Grooms: Gay and Bisexual Husbands in Straight Marriages;* and *Over the Cliff: Gay Husbands in Straight Marriages.*